WHITE FOLKS BE TRIPPIN':

An Ethnography Through Poetry & Prose

Cover Design by:

Jermaine Benton & Sean Marion of Iconevie.com

ISBN #: 978-1-71675-863-8

Table of Contents

White folks
be like
scared
of saying
the wrong thing

Black folks
be like
scared
of dying
for being Black

Yet we
be like
trying to have
conversations
like this shit is
normal

Just in case we don't know each other already, my name is J Mase III. Yes, J Mase is really my first name. Yes, you have to call me that with your whole chest. This book exists because a few years ago, I moved from NYC to the city of Seattle in the Pacific Northwest and well...shit got weird. It got different. It got...white. I mean hella, hella, hella white. I knew there were white people in the world, but I just didn't know how many and to what extent. As Black, Brown & Indigenous folks, we often have to be experts on whiteness to survive work, and getting housing, and just navigating this whole system of American Imperial mediocrity. But being a whole Black Trans person living in the PNW? Well, now I'm a super expert. And as such, I thought I'd write an anthropological account of sorts. An Ethnography. A study of all the white ass shit I have observed here and throughout the course of my adult life, cause why not? Hell, they do it to us and make buttloads of money and crush whole civilizations. So, sit back, relax and take in a poem, a rant or just be with your thoughts in a space committed to exposing the realities of whiteness.

White folks becoming "educated" about racism is not the same as them being committed to undoing racism and white supremacy. The education of white people is not my ministry.

White Folks Dancing in Their Natural Habitat

This is a poem dedicated to white tears
and to offbeat awkward dancing that is
unashamed
of how much space it can truly take up
This poem is white
white like paper
white like the police officers watching the
way I walk
white like university presidents
white like mayonnaise
white like the cast of Friends
white like bleach
white like appropriating slang from
neighborhoods it'd never even want to touch
white like a gay pride parade in Salt Lake City
or a Seattle Solstice
white like "I just wanted to play Devil's
advocate for a second"
This poem is Snow White

it quotes Disney movies
and loooooves it some damn Miley Cyrus
This poem wants you to teach it how to
twerk
this poem has once dated a Black person
and wants you to know it
Especially after it has started sentences with
phrases like
"Not to be racist, but"
This poem has a job
at Bank of America
or Amazon
or maybe Apple
with a 401k and thinks you need to pay for
your own damn healthcare
even though my Black ancestors

paid for the building that its cubicle sits in
with their lives
This poem wants to move to the city to rebel
but will move back to the suburbs when it
starts making little haikus

This poem holds its arms up to blue ink after
taking vacations on colonized land and says
"look, I'm almost as dark as you"
This poem just took a gap year
This poem shares YouTube videos of Jon
Oliver talking about race
cause white boys talking about race are the
only experts on race
this poem will recognize
This poem is a democrat but has a few
republican friends
just to be diverse
This poem loves the word *diverse*
This poem gets lonely because it's not sure if
it has a culture
This poem takes no responsibility
for your oppression
It's not this poem's fault that it was made on
high grade paper...
This poem is vanilla
without all the complications of the Middle
Passage that put that extract in your
Grandma's favorite recipe

This poem is Bugs Bunny circa 1965
This poem is deeply invested in anti-racism
unless that means it doesn't get to be in
charge
This poem wants to talk about its pain with
you
cause it's *like*, **hard** to be oppressive
This poem thinks Rachel Dolezal is a national
treasure
This poem will want to process its feelings
with you later after this poet is done
This poem refuses to acknowledge the color
of the ivory paper that it's printed on
This poem agrees with your politics but not
your tactics
This poem wants you to know that
#AllStanzasMatter
and that we are all really just poems
whether we are sonnets or slam
It has a Bernie Sanders brand necktie
and a Hillary Clinton decoupage on its
nightstand

This poem is so white it knows what
decoupage means
and believes yes, we can change the world
one poem at a time
as long as white poems
with the "right" politics
get to hit the stage **first**

And what of the "good" white people? The ones that separate themselves from the pack. The ones that turn their noses down at the other(s) white people. What happens to them when they realize, they are the exact same white people we're always talking about?

Love Black
People more
than you love
virtue
signaling.

A Rant About White Power Structures Disguised as Do-Gooders (feat. Ambiguous Power Guy)

If you've been paying attention, you know that white folks have a lot of motherfucking audacity. They treat Black, Brown & Indigenous folks as an afterthought, even when they state their intentions are to work towards racial justice. We are their muses, but rarely their leaders. Let's get into what that actually looks like in the world.

A few years back I made a tool to talk about what power typically looks like here in the US. Because I still don't know a better way to illustrate it, we're going to dust off my artistic skills and drift into some imagination space. Okay?

We're starting here with this very lovely humanoid I have carefully and exactingly drawn into a computing device of some kind:

This handsome creature, I call Ambiguous Power Guy. Why Ambiguous Power Guy, not Person, or humxn or something more gender neutral? Well, because patriarchy is real and we gotta be honest about our shit.

So, next, what we want to do with this lovely, is we want to imagine the typical Bank CFO, University President or member of Congress...When we think of these roles let's name the typical social identities the Ambiguous Power Guy embodies. We'll use this naming to fill in APG to complete the image. (Note: When I am saying social identities, I mean identities and experiences that tie this person to legacies of other people. For example, their race/class/gender and not their condescending tone of voice.) I did part of the work here:

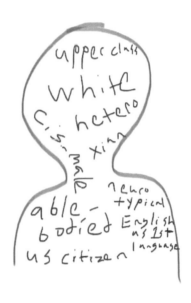

In the very real possibility that you can't read my handwriting, I'll name a few of the things I put in here. (This is by no means an exhaustive list, but rather a starting place.) I wrote white, cis, able-bodied, US citizen, English as a 1st language, neurotypical, upper class, hetero, and Xian (Christian). Other identities that might come up could be middle aged, wealthy, graduate degree, and no criminal record (note this designation doesn't mean they've never committed crimes, but rather they have the ability to not be labeled as a criminal).

When we witness this filled in APG, I am hoping we can acknowledge that this is usually what power looks like in the US. Privilege in this instance is then of course being able to observe the people in power and saying, "Hey, there are some parts of my identity and/or experience the folks in power have in mind when they are making decisions." It can also be about your proximity to these. For example, if you identify as a Black/Brown/Indigenous person, but you are light skinned and/or pass as white that matters. As a Black Trans person, I am also masculine of center in a world that favors masculinity. I deal with transantagonism and transphobia, but in a way that is often different than my Trans feminine siblings.

Is this making sense to you? Good.

Next, we're going to take a professional field to look at more closely: non-profits. Why non-profits? Because I think that they are greatly misunderstood, and because I worked at quite a few and consistently saw the same problems. When you think about the word non-profit, what do you imagine? What feelings are evoked within you? Lots of people think fluffy do-gooder vibes. However, is that true? Non-profits are a government categorization and being registered as one has no actual bearing on the intent of the founders/agents operating that entity. (Remember, the National Football League was a registered non-profit up until 2015.)

Let's get even more specific. When we think about non-profits that deal with the environment, who do we see running them? Are the folks running them more likely to be the working class, Black/Brown/Indigenous folks most impacted by climate change? Or, are they going to look more like the folks already in power like APG? That's rhetorical of course. If you live in the West, there's a reason we have been conditioned to see saving the environment devoid of the people who are currently fighting climate change for their lives. If these environmental organizations don't take their leadership cues from folks who are experts in the problem, how can they actually come up with efficient workable solutions? Answer: They can't.

They're not set up to. They do however, gain social and monetary capital off the labor, knowledge and legacy of those most at risk.

What about mainstream non-profits who deal with LGBTQIA issues? If we commit ourselves to the fact that those most impacted by anti-LGBTQIA violence are Black Trans Women & Femmes, are immigrants, are disabled folks, are working class folks, folks who are constantly policed, does leadership within LGBTQIA organizations reflect that? What does the leadership at mainstream LGBTQIA orgs tend to look like? Mostly they look like white, cis, able-bodied folks with graduate degrees sitting tucked away in board rooms. So, if that's what leadership at organizations like the HRC, GLSEN, the Task Force, etc look like...how can they be invested in ending violence against Black Trans Women & Femmes? How can they be invested in closing the racialized wealth gap? How can they support those in community who are harassed by police? If they weren't born from and don't center leaders who are most impacted by anti-LGBTQIA violence, how can they actually know what problems need to be most urgently addressed? They truly don't. Through grants, donations and feel good ad placements with sponsors, they profit off the stories and work of folks most impacted while only viewing them as an after-thought...as a note to return to in their 10 year plan somewhere.

Have you experienced orgs that gaslit you like that? Had you all believing in a mission that really just turned out to be making white folks feel good about their choice of work or donation practices? Let me tell y'all, after years of working at white organizations that offered nothing more to their Black employees than a headache and a mediocre hand shake, I've learned a lot.

One thing I learned, is that there should be a name given to the voice** white women use in the workplace when they disagree with you, but also see you as too incompetent to know better.

Surprise Writing Exercise!! Name that voice!!

_____

_____

_____

_____

_____

_____

_____

Another thing I learned, is that white folks will spend way more time trying to bait you into circular conversations about race that go nowhere and wonder why you left. They will underpay you, call you combative when you speak up about the racism you're experiencing and white tears you under the table.

Well, damn. Now I am imagining all the places white folks have cried in my presence at work. Not because of what I did or said mind you, but because they have unresolved shit they ain't work out yet in their spirits or with their ancestors. I have had white folks cry after I told them a meeting space was just for Black/Brown/Indigenous folks. I have had white folks cry because I told them their thoughts about Trayvon Martin were irrelevant. I have had white folks cry because I said something they said was racist. I have had white folks cry because they never saw the Wiz (which truthfully is the only valid reason to cry in this pile). I have had white folks cry because I was held up by the police and even though they personally took it upon themselves to forgive the police, it was very emotional for them to know what I had just gone through on their watch. White folks love using Black folks to access their emotions. White tears is a way that they pull up all that trapped guilt like a loogie they are about to spit out. Yes, white tears are gross.

List ways you've seen white tears waste the time, energy of and/or be weaponized against Black people specifically:

_____

_____

_____

_____

We are not all fighting for the same thing and we need to be honest about that. Some of us are fighting to be part of white systems. Some of us are fighting to abolish white supremacy all together. Some are fighting to seem like good people.

Motives are important because the end goal says a lot about how hard and long folks are planning to be in the fight with you.

I don't trust anyone who demands peace of people that are being terrorized.

The Non-Violent Zombie Apocalypse (aka Jesus, MLK & a Zombie Walk Into a Bar...)

There are at least four facts about Jesus and Martin Luther King Jr that I know to be very true:

1. They were both deeply committed to non-violent resistance
2. They were both killed for their public resistance to the state
3. They are both clearly zombies
4. I will always get attacked for number three

Logged Evidence #1
Jesus lay dead in a tomb for three days
and rose triumphantly from his gravesite
to spread his message of forever lasting life
Famous for saying things like "turn the other cheek"

Logged Evidence #2
Martin Luther King Jr was shot through the
right cheek and down through the spinal cord
on April 4th, 1968.
Yet, somehow
despite the death of his physical body
he still keeps speaking.
Only these days,
he seems to only speak through white people
that conjure him up any time I start to sound
a little too
angry about police
or prisons
or the wealth gap
also known as racism

They make his mouth move in directions
a dead body shouldn't be accustomed to
Yet he is always forming new opinions
with statements like
"Martin Luther King would disagree"
"Martin Luther King would have thought you
should be nicer…"

"King would want you to stay nonviolent..."
For some reason his transition has made him
speak in third person

Curious
Our ancestor known in life for his dedication
to Black liberation
has somehow become the servant to white
people's dreams
the rotting of his flesh
seems to make him even more attractive to
white supremacist puppeteers
wanting me to really hone in on the message

See I was told once
that zombies were a warning tale among
slaves
That even if you were to escape the cursed
life of slavehood
through death
your master may still have dominion over
your soul
and your body still forced to do his bidding

I remember these stories
whenever I hear someone holding up my
dead ancestor's mouth
and propping him up to speak

It is a warning
that says
Here is your leader
We have killed him
He says what we want him to now
Careful
it doesn't
happen to you

Stop using dead Black bodies
against the living
and calling it nonviolent
My liberation is not in the past
Many of us are still waiting
for freedom
And I don't want my goal to be dead by 39

Know this
The same people
who will want to placate you
around the death of your fallen
are the same
as the people that would dance on your
grave

I am not waiting for my enemy
to reveal itself
It is already dancing with my
ancestor's body in the streets
and will be broadcast on tonight's evening
news
as I watch more Black activists
being beaten with
the memory of ancestor
forced into zombiehood
by the same system waiting for us all to die
So they can tell the world
what they really wanted us to say
And leave our descendants left to wonder
Who was really fighting for them anyway

It takes more than weapons to colonize a people. It takes destroying their collective memory. It takes destroying their knowledge of all they have accomplished and taking away their rights to dream/hope/envision. The false idols we have of white slave masters in towns and cities across this land matters. Turning folks like MLK into a zombie speaking only in the interests of white peace matters. The twisting of Black organizers' rhetoric and tactics matters. It's a war cry and it has been sounding a long time.

Jobs white people invented to profit off the history, labor and/or bodies of Black/Brown/Indigenous folks while simultaneously devaluing them:

Explorer

Anthropologist

Art Historian

Museum Curator

Social Services

Pope

Wall Street Trader

Missionary

Medical Researcher (Henrietta Lacks deserved better and James Marion Sims was a piece of shit.)

Non-Profit Everything

Peace Corps Volunteer

Fashion Designer

Additions to this list:

_____

_____

_____

_____

_____

_____

_____

_____

_____

_____

It's very cruel to say that you are analytical and need more stats/figures to prove racism exists. You're not more rational than Black/Brown/ Indigenous folks, you're just the beneficiary of violent behavior.

Words and/or Phrases You Only Use to Communicate With White Folks:

_____

_____

_____

_____

_____

_____

_____

_____

_____

_____

_____

_____

_____

_____

_____

Listennnnnn, Shakespeare made up over 400 words and white people love Shakespeare. So, Black folks, don't even bother feeling imposter syndrome in places that reduce your language and your tongue to being made up or "improper". People are just mad at how quickly our languages can adapt and how slow they are to keep up.

No matter what a CEO tells you, there's no amount of corporate sponsorship that equals justice.

Of COVID Masks and Quarantine
(or FUCK BEN FRANKLIN)

His crusty post read
kinda like a movie
that only incels
would watch

> *"Those who would give up essential Liberty, to*
> *purchase a little temporary Safety, deserve*
> *neither Liberty nor Safety." -Ben Franklin,*

Well, that's according
to the white boy
on Facebook
who wasn't perceptive enough
to cite the irony
of using a slave master's words
to defend human
autonomy.

White boys are funny like that
They tell jokes sometimes
about our existence
but they state it as a matter of fact

Like matter is a fact
based on the observer's perception
Like they don't think you
or I
have the capacity to observe
Like I am just a state of matter
to be acted upon
or observed
They build shrines
to their forefathers
with our hands
And with just a slip of tongue
and slab of concrete
they are no longer war mongers
or colonizers
or rabid cave beasts
They are free thinkers
that somehow
meditated
their way up the food chain
Cause how dare I
as a state of matter
observe them
as a matter of fact
being anything else
but fine examples of

monuments
to dead masters' egos
in alabaster stone waste lands
Free their haircuts
from oppression
Free them from
their need to protest
from their need to wave
their guns
free them from accountability
They aren't looking for justice
just the right to preside
over the world again
unquestioned

Instead of continuing to revamp diversity/inclusion efforts at white orgs to make them better...you could just let them fail. They already have been failing Black/Brown/Indigenous folks
#LetWhitePeopleFail

A few years ago I was giving a sermon at a white church (UU) and afterwards, about 50 folks lined up to tell me how great I spoke, but mostly about all the ways they as white folks in this hella white church were already so great at dealing with racism. This one woman, in her 70's, told me she wanted to do something, but it was just so hard to know what to do (never mind that's what my entire sermon was about). I said, no shade, but do you want your tombstone to read, "Here lies Sally, she lived til 95 and once thought really hard about ending racism."

Repeat after me:

I will not mistake a corporate and/or police photo op for actual solidarity and accountability.

#AllyFail

You are the kind of ally that would rather ask
me how to twerk
than how to pronounce my name
You are the kind of ally that doesn't know
what cisgender means
but loves staring at my chest before you
address me
You are the kind of ally that makes me
wonder who my enemies are
and trips over words
like transphobia and white supremacy
You are the kind of ally that will practice your
sassy Black woman voice in the mirror
but cross the street when actual Black folks
pass by you on street corners
You are the kind of ally that just showed up
to help gay people have fancier weddings
You are the kind of ally that wants to take
pictures together
just for advertising purposes

You are the ally
that calls my family's neighborhood up and
coming
but would never want to bring up the word
gentrification
You are ally on white horse
seemingly scooping down to rescue me from
my own depravities
You are the kind of ally that shops only at
Whole Foods
You are the ally that doesn't realize being gay
won't stop you from having white privilege
You are the ally that tells old Black men how
adorable they are
when they're cleaning your floors
You are the ally that sends me links to social
justice articles you've only read the title to
You are the ally that will think
"Well, gosh, this couldn't possibly be a poem
about me"
You are ally waving righteous sword
that loves to hear me tell a sad story over
and over again

because vicariously living my pain gives you
some street cred
You are the kind of ally that thinks
intersectionality uses too many syllables
You are the ally that loves the texture of my
hair
You are the ally that thinks wanting to fuck
me is somehow the same as fighting for me
You are the ally that celebrates don't ask
don't tell
because kids that look like you will never be
forced to cross seas to bomb kids that look
like them just so they can have some of your
fictitious "freedom"
You are the ally that thinks being accepted is
the same as being understood
You are the ally that laughs way too hard at
my jokes
You are the kind of ally that doesn't
understand the problem with words like
'minorities'
You are the kind of ally that believes being
on food stamps

for your adult Americorps position
is the same as a 10 year old brain eating
itself for nourishment
You are the kind of ally that thinks I talk too
loudly when I am angry
You are the ally that thinks rape is funny
because it hasn't happened to you
You are that ally that thinks saying you are
colorblind is somehow a *compliment?*
You are the ally that thinks believing in
systemic oppression is an option
You are the ally that will fuck up my
pronouns but think it's okay
cause we're like...friends
You are the kind of ally that will need to
appropriate some yoga after this poem
But you be that kind of ally that would only
remember that last line about yoga
in this poem
You are the ally that never has to progress
because you have already proclaimed
yourself to be
my ally

Corporations, universities and non-profits tweeting "Black Lives Matter" does NOT make up for them undermining and underpaying Black people the rest of the year.

Racial justice in education does not mean Black/Brown/Indigenous folks spending the entire day educating white folks on racism and white supremacy. It means we as Black folks, as Brown folks, and as Indigenous folks have a right to learn and deepen our own knowledge. That is an experience often stolen from us and then we are demanded to be of service to others even in many "racial justice" spaces.

When White People Tell Me They Are Progressive

When white people tell me they are
progressive
what I really hear is
"yeah
I smile real big at Black people on the bus
sometimes"
I hear
"My vote really does matter"
I hear
"I like to read the New York Times on the
weekend
and tip my Brown waiter 25% at brunch"
What I don't hear is
familiarity
I see red wine stained teeth
pleading for me to see them as nice people
Nice being the operative word
and far more important than justice

My neighbor calls my new neighborhood in
the Pacific Northwest
"Paradise"
I hear
"Genocide really does work"
I hear
the sound of my sneakers
tip toeing late at night as not to spook my
neighbors'
whitest sensibilities
I hear
blue and yellow garden flowers
I've never been allowed to lay my eyes on til
now
whispering
that I am an intruder into my own home
I hear
Black Muslim teenager pushed off high
building
I hear
white silence
I hear
white noise

Only the tv is the political system
and I can't reach in far enough to turn it
down
I hear
"We're real progressive"
I hear
me screaming to be seen
at white folks
that only see nice
That are more offended by my usage of the
word fuck
then the fact that the police pulled a gun on
me last week for laughing too loud while
Black
I hear
wasted sentiments of "I can't believe that still
happens"
I hear
progressive
as my obituary
I hear
white mouths
spitting the politest of bullshit

thinking their words alone must matter
to me
I see them
eyeing me up
wanting me to recognize them
for their virtues
Anger is a fucking virtue
It is a survival technique
I forged the vilest of my ire
with the help of my dead ancestors
that Becky's nice progressive grandparents
killed off years ago
I planted it far beyond Pluto
So even the most committed of colonizers
can't gentrify it yet
"I see no color"
They spew
In the whitest of board rooms
In their ivory cul de sacs
In their book clubs
and preaching about white Jesus from their
Sunday morning pews
"We're all working for the same thing"

they say
while blocking the path to my entry
I hear
the median access to wealth for a white
woman in the US
is $42,500
and that for a Black woman in the same
country it is only 500 bucks
Yet I hear progressives
spending more time talking about their fragile
white feelings
and corporate candidates
than the redistribution of their own stolen
wealth
I hear
"Black people are so angry"
I wear that shit like a vest
Cause ain't no one gonna tell me
liberal fantasies ain't dangerous
I ain't your Tulsa Oklahoma
I ain't your Saartjie Baartman
I ain't the Tubman on your $20 bill
I'm still alive to call you on your shit

And trust
It Is My Duty
To Fire back
Assalamualaikum

When I hear the word "inclusion" I hear white folks wanting Black people to disappear into their organizations and their dreams instead of understanding that Black people have a right to autonomy and mutually beneficial collaboration.

White Supremacy Wants to Be Your Friend on Facebook

White Supremacy does not care who you
voted for
who your parents marched with
or what your nickname was in school
It wants to destroy
It wants to wrap its fingers around your
throat
and use your voice to make its case
It's just so easy
It just wants to be friends
Wants you to take it to dinner parties and
crack jokes
It wants you to worry about what those other
white folks think
It wants you to care more about order
than about Black & Brown survival
It wants you to play nice
to act sweet

to ask, why do you have to be so damn
angry?
White Supremacy is in your blood
it curved itself around your little red cells
and plays with your heartbeat to the point
that you don't even really know what you
believe
You just want to be easy
...be easy
be likeable
mean people don't have friends
people that attack White Supremacy
well... they're mean
unkind
loud
aggressive
they just don't speak right
they're manipulative
White Supremacy is nice
puts bad people in jail
keeps mean people from getting jobs at
establishments with pretty signs

it plants flowers outside of banks that owned
your ancestors
but wouldn't dare dream of giving you a loan
it keeps those kinds of people broke
it rewards the hard work of those who keep
their damn mouths closed
keep your damn mouth closed
it's a secret
this can be our secret
don't you want nice things?
don't make people too uncomfortable
White Supremacy hates when you make
people think about unpleasant things
we just want to get along
let's be that melting pot we talked about
extend your hand
not everyone needs a voice here
not everyone needs to have feelings
we don't have feelings
we have White Supremacy
White Supremacy tells us how to feel
and right now

it tells us that the feeling of the day is that
your life just don't matter
Stop pushing the issue
there is no issue here
be easy
take it
swallow it down
if you play the right rules
we'll pretend to give you power
we may kill your entire family
but you will be the exception
we will pretend to love you
White Supremacy wants us to pretend to love
you
while killing off everything you have ever
known to love
let us teach you our language
let us give you our version of history
the right version of events
so you forget
how great you felt when you actually
mattered
the rewards will be amazing

though you may not be around to receive
them
because White Supremacy wants them to go
through us first
it wants us to tell you your turn is coming
White Supremacy will make just enough
space
for you to get discouraged by the game
White Supremacy wants you to give up
We'll help you
White Supremacy wants to know if this threat
has been eliminated
I mean has your spirit been eliminated
I mean has your drive to circumvent been
eliminated
I mean has your will to survive been
eliminated
I mean has your soul been eliminated
If the answer to these questions is yes
then we want to know
if you'd like to be Our friend
White Supremacy has already sent you a
request

If you're smart
then perhaps someday
you'll just learn to go ahead
and click
on accept]

Ways we are trained to protect white innocence:

_____

_____

_____

_____

_____

_____

_____

_____

_____

_____

_____

_____

_____

_____

_____

_____

I have never met an adult over 25 that hasn't committed a crime. Yet, I am clear, only some of us will ever be criminalized.

Dealing with White Folks During the Holy Month

I've spent some time co-running a group for incarcerated Trans & Queer youth. I started my b-day yesterday by picking up a few supplies before heading to the detention center with a colleague to see off one of our kids who is being released today. He is 12 & closeted. I was tasked w/ picking up a few things we thought he might enjoy & called my colleague through the process because I was having anxiety about what might be appropriate. We settled on his favorite snacks and a stuffed unicorn. I was worried he wouldn't like it/would feel like it was too "kiddy" or maybe too "gay". But it was adorable and if he didn't like it we had the snacks. So, as I was mulling this over having missed Suhoor that morning and being without food all day I was a little foggy, emotional, all the things (#RamadanProblems). I got to the cash register and the cashier was a white woman I had never seen before (the store is in my neighborhood and I am there fairly frequently for supplies). She saw the unicorn & remarked how cute it was. I relayed my nervousness about giving a stuffed unicorn to a 12 year old who is on the cusp of thinking it is either really cool or really ridiculous for his age. She asked a question, that had I had some food in my system I would have answered very differently. She asked, "What's the occasion?" In the part of my brain that usually says "random white strangers are great at dehumanizing Black/Brown children, just lie and be done with ya day", I wanted to tell her "It's his birthday!" But I didn't say that because that part of my brain was severely lacking calories & foresight. So I paused. I long paused. I paused so long that if there was a physical manifestation of that pause it would be a 5K run for making better decisions. After pausing, I told the truth, "Oh, he is getting out of a detention center." Her response was typical of someone who's gotten to see the "justice system" humanize them their entire life & quickly says, "I hope he learned his little lesson". A few other parts of my brain lit up and I growled back: "I hope they stop incarcerating children." I took the unicorn (which he loved) & left. It's painful to know the many ways whiteness tries to rob even our kids of joy.

When have you witnessed moments that Black/Brown/Indigenous children were robbed of the right to be honored as kids:

_____

_____

_____

_____

_____

_____

_____

_____

_____

_____

_____

_____

_____

_____

_____

_____

_____

_____

Academia is always 10 years behind the lived reality of the folks on the ground. Prioritizing articles and textbooks over real people's collective experiences is one way to avoid accountability for the current world we live in.

White people
love titles
They will call
you essential
before they
will give you a
paycheck.

Think back to a workplace argument with a white co-worker or boss. What SHOULD you have said? Win the argument through a poem:

_____

_____

_____

_____

_____

_____

_____

_____

_____

_____

_____

_____

_____

_____

_____

_____

_____

_____

_____

The reason I don't trust white folks to do racial justice work alone, is instead of actually reallocating resources they end up in long philosophical debates about language. If your uncle John drops the n word at Sunday dinner but y'all both living off slave money, how y'all different?

On Naming (whiteness)

There's these moments where you're having such a great conversation on the internet in Black/Brown/Indigenous space and a white person leaves a comment so off the wall they may as well have just typed "FISHSTICKS!!!" and called it a day...So, I've started yelling FISHSTICKS at confused white folks meandering without purpose in their neighborhoods. As I continue my study of these creatures, I'm certain there must be other names for white folks in the lexicon I have yet to discover...Like, the non-majestic alabaster cave beast. The thin-lipped Kraft mac & cheese eater. Mayonnaise tester. The Mr. Rogers looking non-negro. The blue veined primate. The devil's beta. More research is clearly needed on this topic.

Random Observations on whiteness (a long ass list):

Folks that won't spend 5 minutes on Google expect Black folks to spend 12 hrs gathering information and detailing painful personal experiences that they will never read.

White folks just be
walking around
with no lips
just mad at the world
peeling in the sun
foaming at the mouth
acting like we don't belong here

White folks just be
telling on themselves
crying about the fucked-up shit they did
telling you

like you supposed to
forgive them

If a white person is from
California
or Canada
they'll tell you 5 million reasons
why they never learned racism where they
grew up
never mind the racism that you've
experienced
exactly where they were birthed
the anti-Blackness
right in the soil
clearly it's not racism
they've never heard of that

I was invited to sell chapbooks, and someone
asked "what is this book about?" I said,
"white supremacy in queer spaces" and they
came back with "oh, you're preaching to the
choir here." And I responded, "how can that

be when I am the only Black person here?"
Silence
White folks love pretending they're the version of themselves they spend all day pontificating about.

Let white folks feel guilty sometimes. That might be the first time they have ever genuinely felt anything for Black/Brown/Indigenous people.

The US government sure did understand reparations when it was paying white slave owners for freeing their slaves.

Sometimes I stop people in the middle of a story and ask, "Does your one Black friend know that you got them in your mouth this much?"

Let's be clear, the only radical thing a major corporation can do in this moment is not to yell "Black Lives Matter". It would be to dissolve themselves and put resources back into the workers and the communities that made their wealth.

White politicians in the year 2020 really thought they could vote against Black interests consistently, but shine it up by kneeling in some kente cloth.

According to many state laws, it's illegal to profit off any publicity related to crimes you have committed. Yet, somehow there is a whole mess of white folks making money off talking about the racism and white supremacy culture they have participated in.

Every time you call someone a "minority" a fairy loses its wings.

You know that part in a white movie where there are absolutely no Black people on screen but suddenly, you hit a huge emotional crescendo or someone is trying to signal they are "cool" and the soundtrack is at full volume stealing the voice from a Black person's throat? If art imitates life, I wonder how often Black folks and culture are used to give white people access to their own emotions in real life...

When white folks say things like, "Even as a white person I agree...", what are they expecting afterwards? A cookie? A high five? Like...is their approval supposed to change my material reality somehow, or...?

If y'all don't learn to capitalize the "B" in Black...☹ ☹ ☹

Wouldn't it be great if instead of interjecting themselves into every conversation about race, white folks acknowledged how painfully far behind they are in their understanding, to the point of derailing truly productive conversations
...and just...
observed...

It is too late in the game to be focused on polite conversations. Either you are about moving resources to Black, Brown & Indigenous communities or you are not about racial justice.

As I finish writing this book, dedicated to Black folks, Brown folks and Indigenous folks who have had to deal with the absurdities of whiteness, across the US and the world, we are witnessing a Black Uprising. So much of this book has been about poking fun at the shit we have to deal with in order to survive as Black people. I want us to end by meditating on what gifts of transformation we envision for our collective future. What follows next is a worksheet for Black people and Black people alone.

What transformational gifts do you want Black folks to experience as part of our Collective Future?

(Draw or Write)

The world you
are fighting for,
beyond
oppression, is
possible. Believe it.
Know it. Hold it as
sacred.

On the shirt: Dear Trans Person, Don't let these cis people gaslight you today, okay?

J Mase III is a Black/Trans/queer poet & educator based in Seattle by way of Philly. As an educator, J Mase has worked with community members in the US, UK, and Canada on the needs of LGBTQIA+ folks and racial justice in spaces such as K-12 schools, universities, faith communities and restricted care facilities. He is founder of awQward, the first trans and queer people of color talent agency.

J Mase is the award-winning author of ***And Then I Got Fired: One Transqueer's Reflections on Grief, Unemployment & Inappropriate Jokes About Death*** and of course ***White Folks Be Trippin': An Ethnography Through Poetry & Prose.***

Currently, he is head writer for the theatrical production ***Black Bois*** and co-editor of ***the***

Black Trans Prayer Book.

He has shared stages with artists such as Lady Dane Figueroa Edidi, Chuck D, MJ Rodriguez, Billy Porter, the Indigo Girls and more. His work and musings have been featured on and in MSNBC, theGrio, the Root, the New York Times, TEDx, Atlanta Black Star, Wear Your Voice as well as Teen Vogue among others.

Find him on Instagram (@jmaseiii) and www.jmaseiii.com!